Touching the Landscape Within

Deborah Alston Wroblewski

WEEPING WILLOW BOOKS

Published by
Weeping Willow Books
Santa Fe NM

www.weepingwillowbooks.com
info@weepingwillowbooks.com

ISBN 979-8-9886688-2-4
Library of Congress Control Number: 2026934747

Interior and cover design by Don Mitchell

Cover painting by Deborah Alston Wroblewski

Back cover photo by Katherine Milham

For Todd

Thank you for guiding me to the place where I don't need permission to breathe.

FOREWORD

I congratulate Deborah on her strength and courage in revisiting her personal challenges, emotions, and thoughts to find resolve and acceptance in dealing with a lifelong congenital issue. She teaches us all the importance of looking within oneself to self-reflect. Thank you, Deborah, for teaching me early in my career to recognize the importance of the mind and soul in treating physical problems. It has been a true honor for you to trust me as your surgeon.

David A. Mattingly, M.D.

Emeritus Orthopedic Chairman, Surgeon in Chief and Aufranc Fellowship Director
New England Baptist Hospital, Boston, MA

Unlocking the Gait

In the account that follows I am going to tell you how a woman became lost and then found due to a mistake, an oversight, probably by a well-meaning doctor, that determined the course of her life. I am that woman. I am seventy-two now and still working to transcend and understand this early trauma of congenital hip dysplasia discovered too late.

I remember the first time I felt sad, even hopeless. I knew something was very wrong. This would not be unusual except that I was less than two years old. The year was 1954. My small body was encased in a plaster cast that extended from armpits to ankles. Days before I was a smiling, happy toddler holding myself up by the rails of the playpen. I knew only joy. I quickly learned about pain, imprisonment, separation, ridicule, and soldiering on. My confinement lasted one year but didn't end there. This condition deeply affected my mother, father and brother along with all the people who would come to love me in my lifetime. I carried my inner and outer wounds along with their effects, and they influenced every decision, hence forth. I became the girl with the odd gait, the disability, that then defined me.

These are the poems that piece together my story.

Mother
two trembling hands
reached out to hold
her child
soft baby skin beneath a hard plaster shell
her heart wept
then hardened.

Touching someone
was difficult for my mother
her mother died young
her first daughter died
she grew a hard shell
I wore a plaster cast
we, in our private cages.

Father
I seek your wise guidance
you said, "Someone will love
you because of it."
Let that someone
be me.

Moving forward
I seek the confidence
you wished for me
harder than you knew.

Shining in the distance
taunting me
is the life I was meant to have
unscathed, undamaged
purely loved and cherished
and in love with
myself.

Walking in shadow
under the streetlights
she saw the uneven gait
that prompted ridicule.
Praying to be straight
and graceful
still it limped
alongside her.

Suddenly seeing
myself shrinking and bowing
I straighten up
and out
and wonder
Why me?

With holy curiosity
I travel back
walking alongside
the girl with
the misshapen bones
and tender heart.

Enabled by her scars
she slowly emerged
to reclaim
all she didn't know
she already possessed.

The breeze at dawn
whispers
*there is still time
you can do this.*

Speaking through longing
I cry out my name
searching the rubble
for the girl
buried beneath.

Feeling bare feet
in the cold sea
I wash my sins
and ask forgiveness
for not knowing
how to be me.

I am seeking
understanding and
acceptance
looking back
to move forward.

She had almost forgotten
how to be happy
carrying her threadbare
blanket of anger
for so long.

Fleeting glimpses
of a happy me
keep me hopeful that
if I work hard enough
she'll stay.

If grace fills empty spaces
may it fill
my hollowed being
with self-love.

For one wild moment
let the whole me and
the damaged me
look each other in the eye
and say *thank you*.

I offer up my quivering soul
forever hoping the shaking
will stop and I
will be held firm
in self-love.

Feeling the signs
that the cage was open
yet I stayed inside
made me realize
I was not yet healed.

Leading me gently
to the time before
my destiny shifted
as the plaster hardened
I ache to reclaim my freedom
my unbridled joy.

I Do

Despite pain and deformity, I became a nurse. I longed to heal, to offer comfort and to spare anyone and everyone from the suffering I had experienced. I did not know then, but my orthopedic condition would make my nursing profession short-lived. Surprisingly, especially to me, I married a young intern. He was a bright man with laser-focused goals. He chose me and I had never been chosen before. I hadn't developed a high opinion of myself and became further lost in marriage, especially after being forced to leave my career due to increasing complications with my joints. I allowed my former feelings of imprisonment and brokenness to follow me into marriage, making it quite a challenge for both of us and the four children that followed. I tried to cope in any way I could, all the while feeling that I was put in yet another type of prison.

Music begins
propelling her forward
I do and I do
I don't see me losing myself
yet, I do

Touching someone
touching him
is difficult when
he dons the armor.
Shining knight, take your armor off
for me.

I appreciate rawness
I ask him to show me
vulnerability
not the clinical coat
of Dr. Husband.

Happily ever after
a fairy tale.
Happy ever?
A childhood game
of hide and seek.
No one comes to find me
not even me.

Love is
more choice
than advertised
more work
than imagined.
Blessed are they
who are easy
to love.

Fleeting glimpses
of happiness in this marriage
make me ponder
can you make a life
of only fleeting glimpses?

Like the best perfume
I cradle the bottle
drinking in the scent of despair
letting it pull me under
tired of fighting.

Lulling the senses
I take my first sip
it lulls, then dulls
taking my pain along with my power.

Something is calling me
to guard my heart
his love is made of words only words
I have been seduced by words.

The breaking of the shell
was not hers to do
it was an inside job.
His.

Touch an intimate sense.
To have and to hold
from this day forward
bewilders us.

Upon my mouth
lay words unspoken
No, I don't want to
No, I don't like that
They shrink like cowards
waving tiny white flags
of surrender.

Acceptance

It took many years, and much soul searching, to realize and understand the chain of events that sealed my fate. I spent decades carrying anger like a battered security blanket. At age seventy-two, I decided I had enough. I looked back to move forward and come to terms with my past and find peace. I began to heal. Our marriage began to heal. I dug deep and found the missing me, the woman who was shaped by the heartbreak of the past but never stopped looking for who she might have been. I found her, she who was made strong, resilient, artistic, imaginative, unconventional, and repaired with gold in the broken places. This is her story, my story.

Shining in the distance
is that resting place
where the before
meets now
and rejoices in their reunion.

I'll tell you
how we became lost so we may find
our way back
together.

This was love
her soul
reuniting
with the pieces
she left behind.

Letting things go
I forgive
not forget
my value
ever again.

First you must realize
that sadness may
always
stay a part of you.
Sing it a lullaby
cradle it in your arms
accept it as your own.

Right now
I pray
my jagged pieces
tumble in the
churning ocean of my life
and become
sea glass.

I sense a knowing
that my real self
is emerging at long last.
If I allowed myself to be present
with all my feelings
I might find I could bear them,
use them as teachers rather than
unwelcome companions,
sit with them and offer tea.

As past, present and future mingle
I feel them all
this day
as I re-enter what is
and leave behind
what might have been.

What version will I settle upon?
everything worked out
or
nothing was as it should be
yet I found a way to
be grateful.

I think every woman is entitled
to know her value
and expect
any man claiming
to love her
know it too.

Touching the landscape
I tread lightly
gingerly respectfully
in this new terrain
of being grateful
in the present.

Taste is different with age
sweeter, softer
ripening
with the warm light of late harvest
in a long marriage.

Taking time
to be thankful
lights
the darkness
within.

With age we understand
the delicate balance of
mourn and savor,
seeing ourselves fading
while fanning the flame.

Discovering a gift
called self-worth
shifts everything into
balance.

The answer
I am seeking
whispers patiently,
acceptance
again, and again.

Acknowledgments

To my husband, Edmund, who calmly traversed what at times was a rough terrain, and for fifty years has held my hand to keep me from falling.

To my brother, Robert, who faced down grade-school bullies for me.

To my daughters Andrea, Katherine and Meredith, and my son, Michael, who never saw me as less than perfect.

To my Philadelphia cousins, Pat Zitter and Sister Denise Amspacher, along with my Aunt Nellie, who spent countless hours visiting me at Temple University Hospital, to give respite to my mother.

To my editor and publisher, Marcia Meier, without whose support and expertise, this book would not exist.

To my writing facilitator, Janet Lucy, for providing me with inspiring prompts to ignite my imagination.

To Dr. David Mattingly, who at New England Baptist Hospital replaced my deformed hips and gave me a miraculous new life beyond pain.

To Santa Barbara Adult Education, which provided me with an artistic outlet to channel pain into painting.

About the Author

Deborah Alston Wroblewski is a former nurse. She is the mother of four, grandmother of eleven, art teacher, artist, writer, and poet whose work explores resilience, pain, love, endurance, and the beauty of imperfection. Her medical condition shaped her life, her art, and soul, but no longer defines her. She gives voice to all women's struggles with body image, marriage, losing oneself, perfectionism, forgiveness, and acceptance. Her memoir in poems seeks to unleash the quiet voice of the silenced woman, the everywoman. She lives in Santa Barbara, California, a long way from her Philadelphia roots, with her husband, Edmund, and cat, Gus, in an old Tudor house near her adult children and many grandchildren. She no longer carries her threadbare security blanket of anger.

Deborah would love to hear from others who experienced congenital hip dysplasia and learn how it affected their lives. You can contact her through Weeping Willow Books at: info@weepingwillowbooks.com